Vintage Botany Prints
Vol. 19

By E. Lawrence

All rights reserved. This book, or parts thereof, may not be reproduced in any form without permission. Images found in this book may have been retouched.

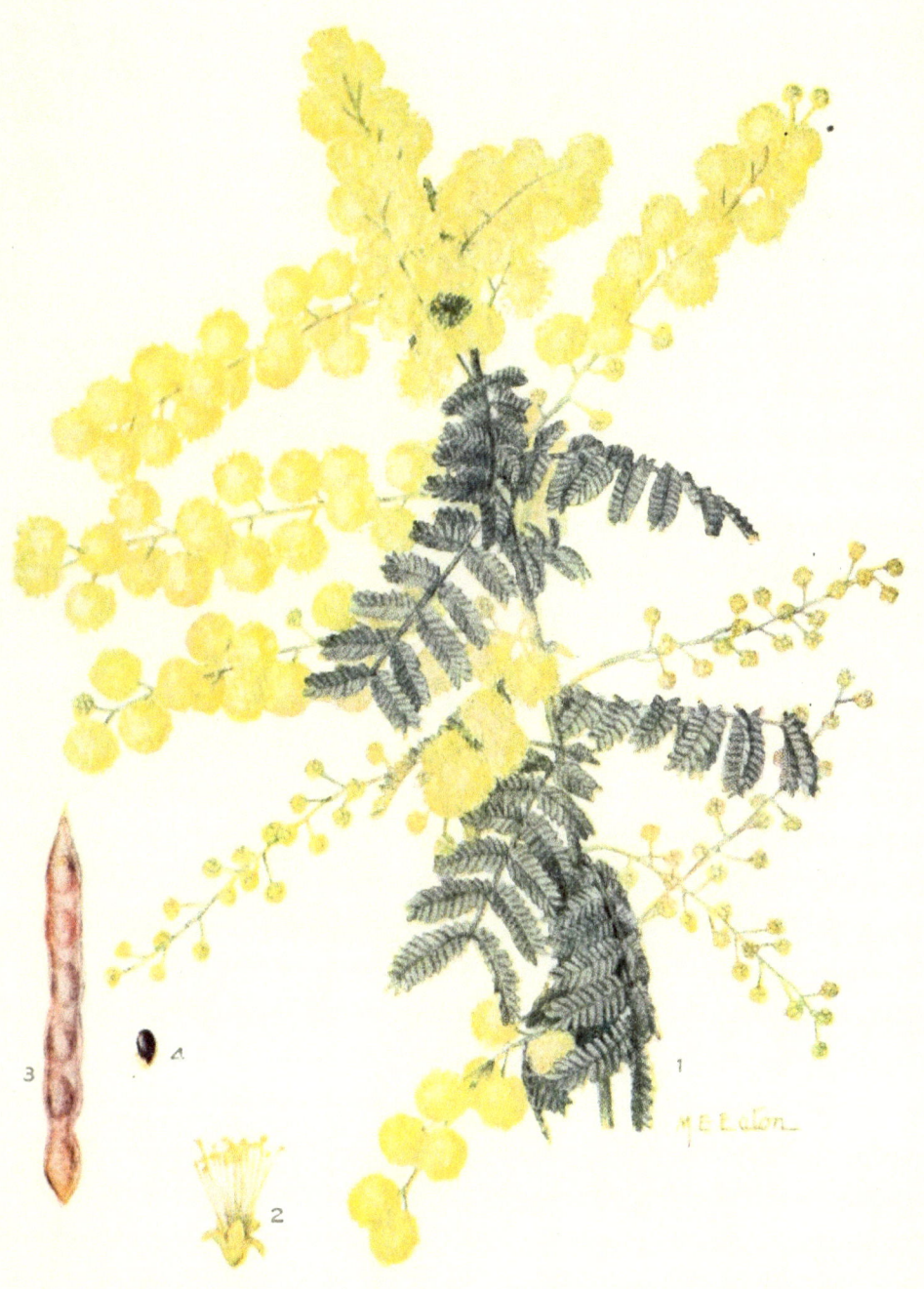

ACACIA PUBESCENS

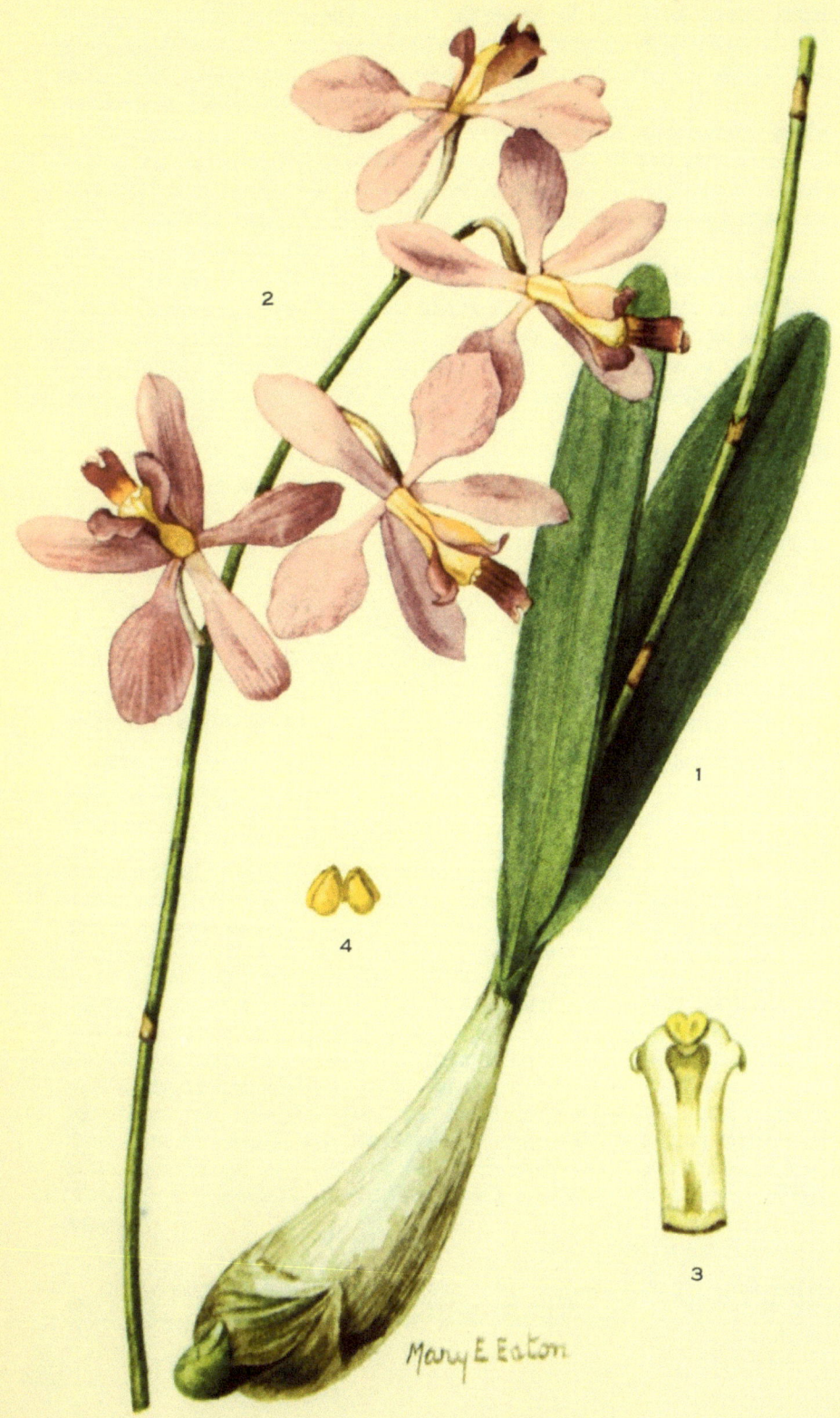

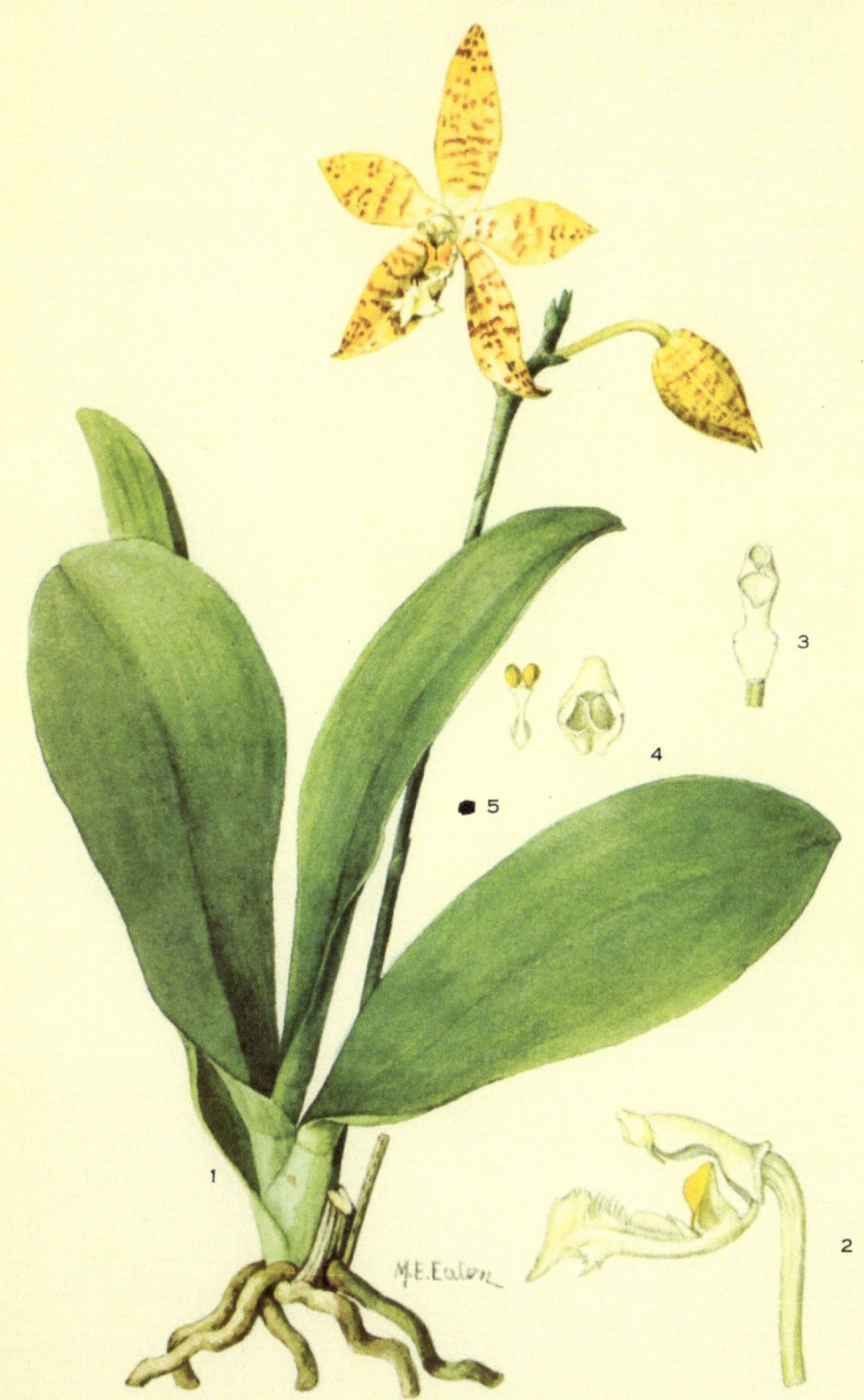

PHALAENOPSIS LUEDDEMANNIANA OCHRACEA

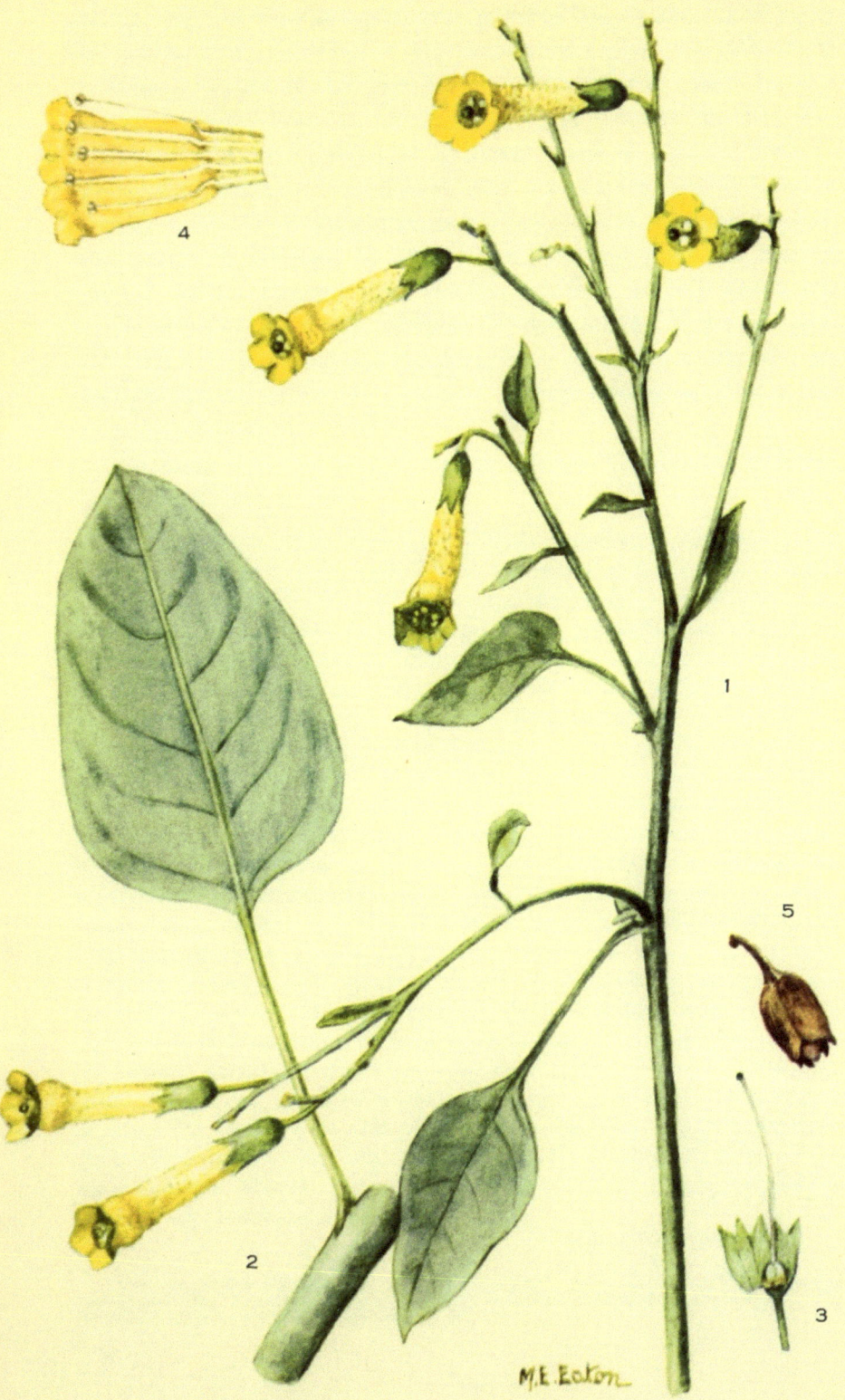

NICOTIANA GLAUCA

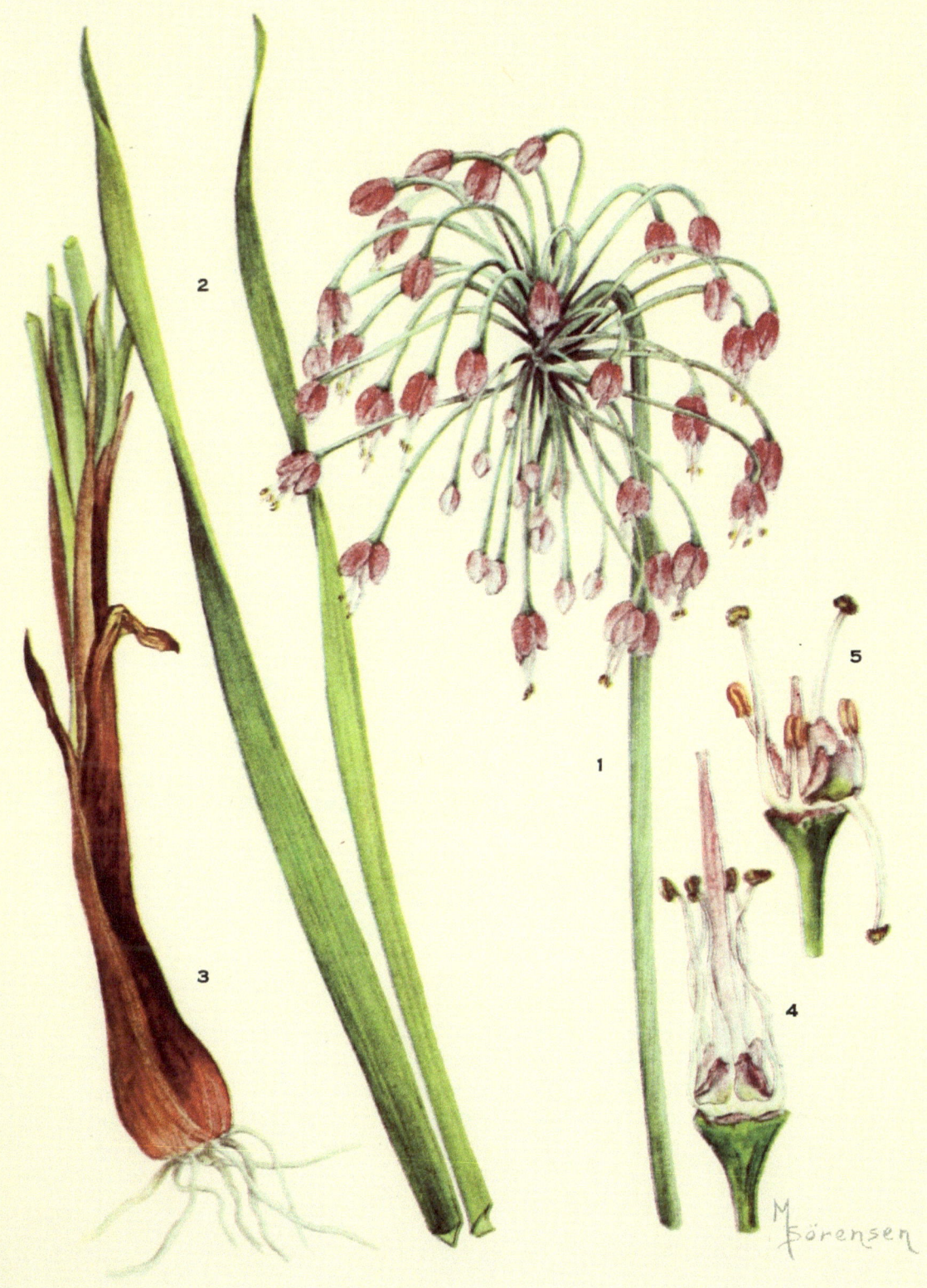

ALLIUM CERNUUM

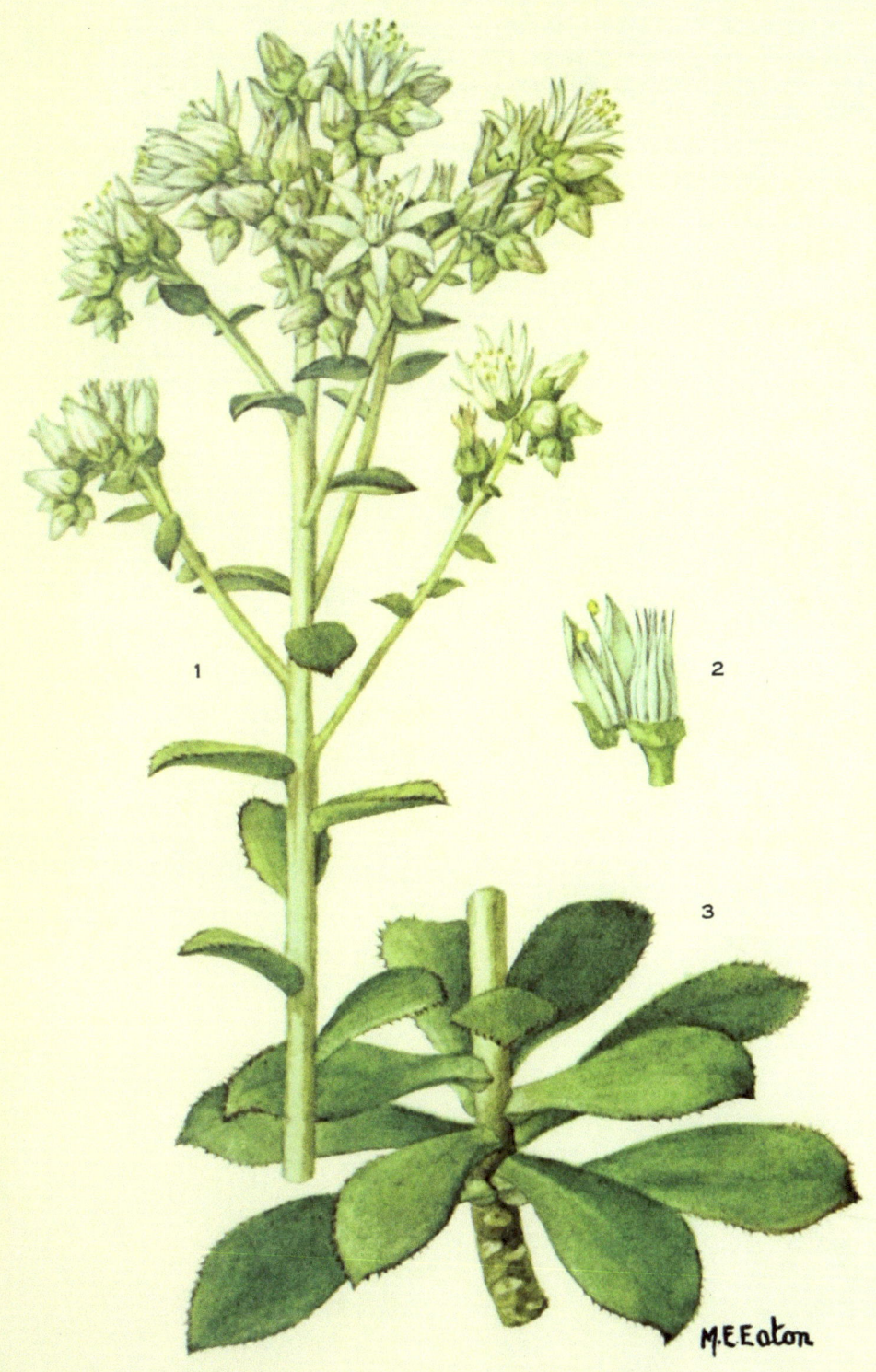

AEONIUM DECORUM

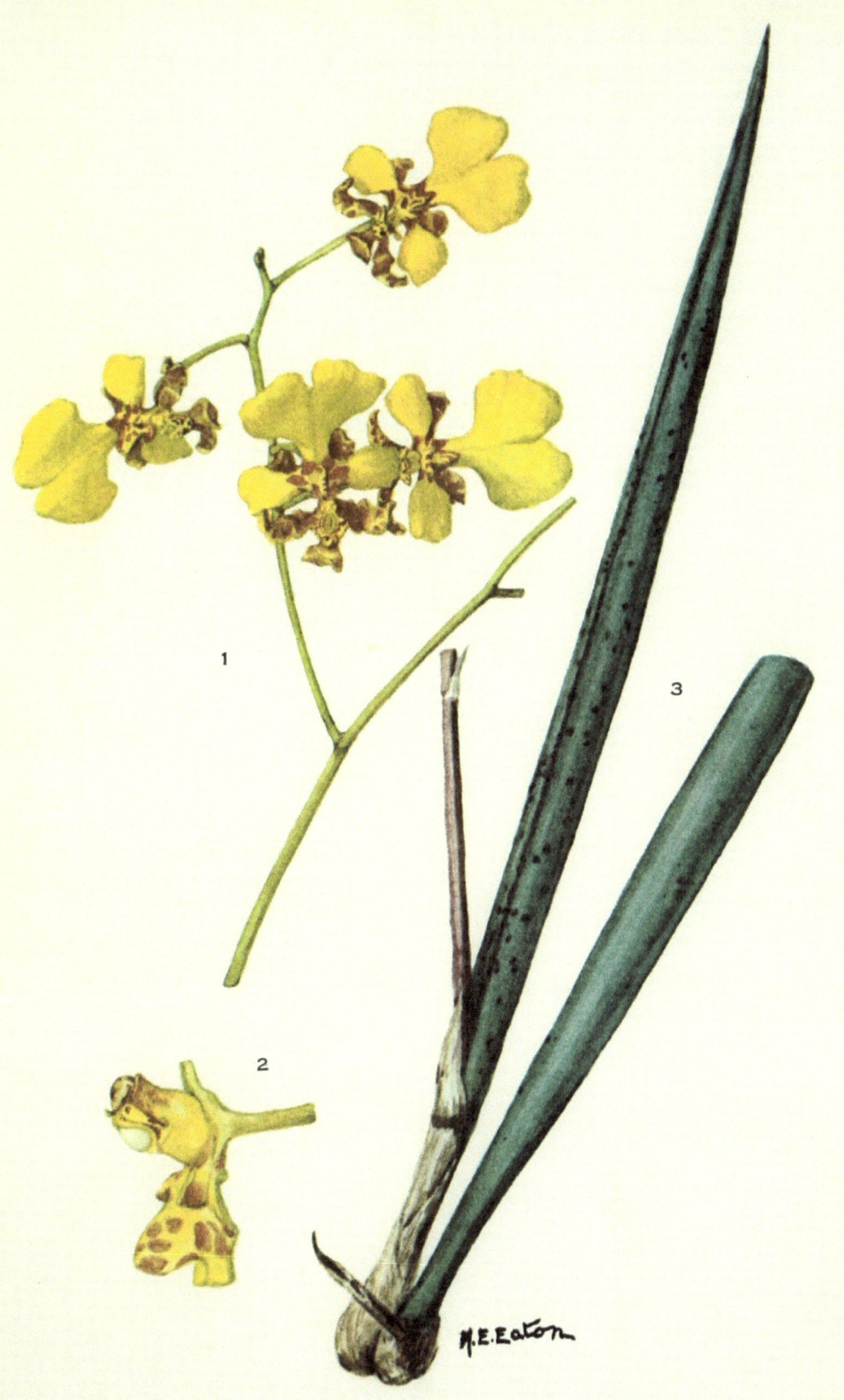

ONCIDIUM CEBOLLETA

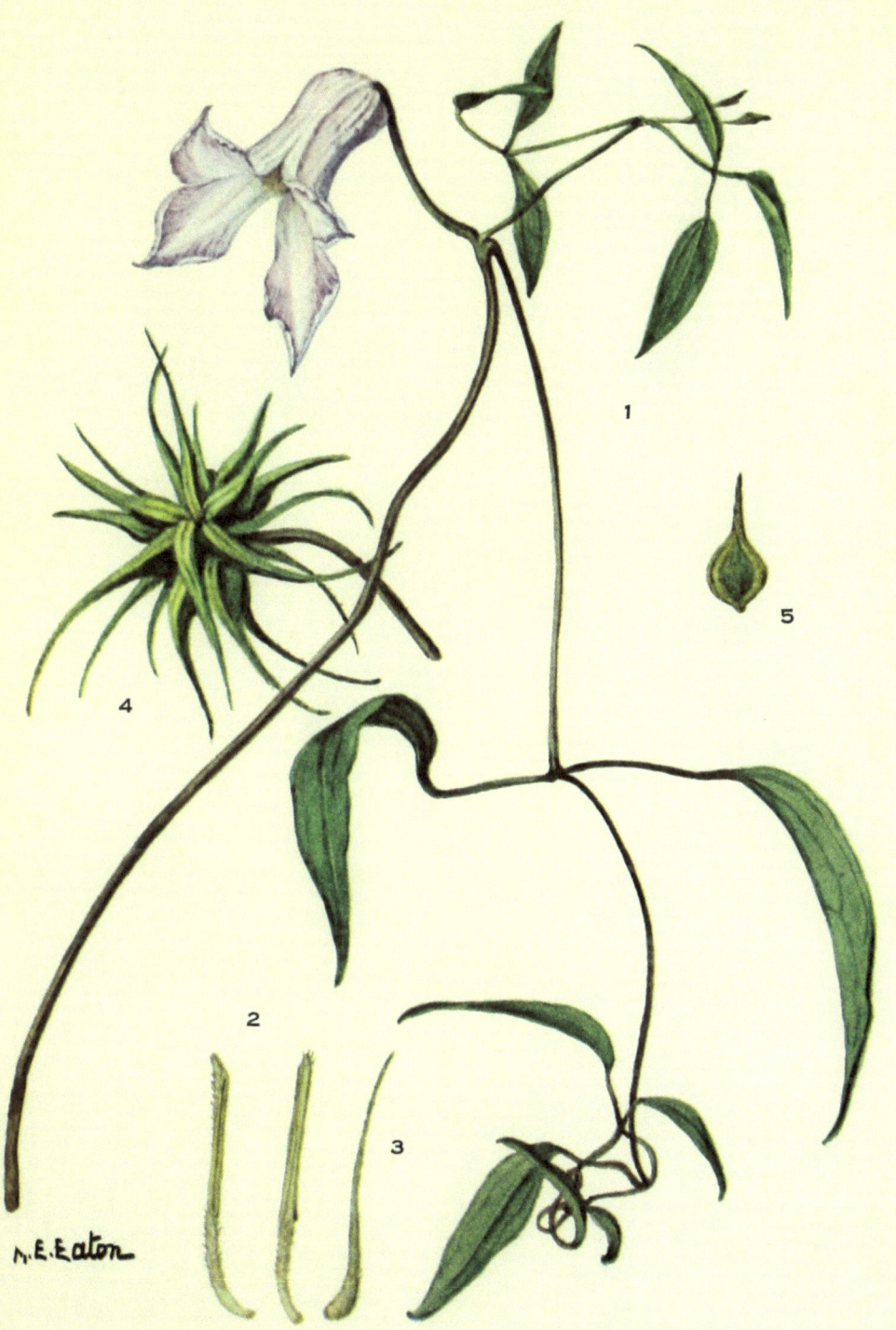

CLEMATIS CRISPA

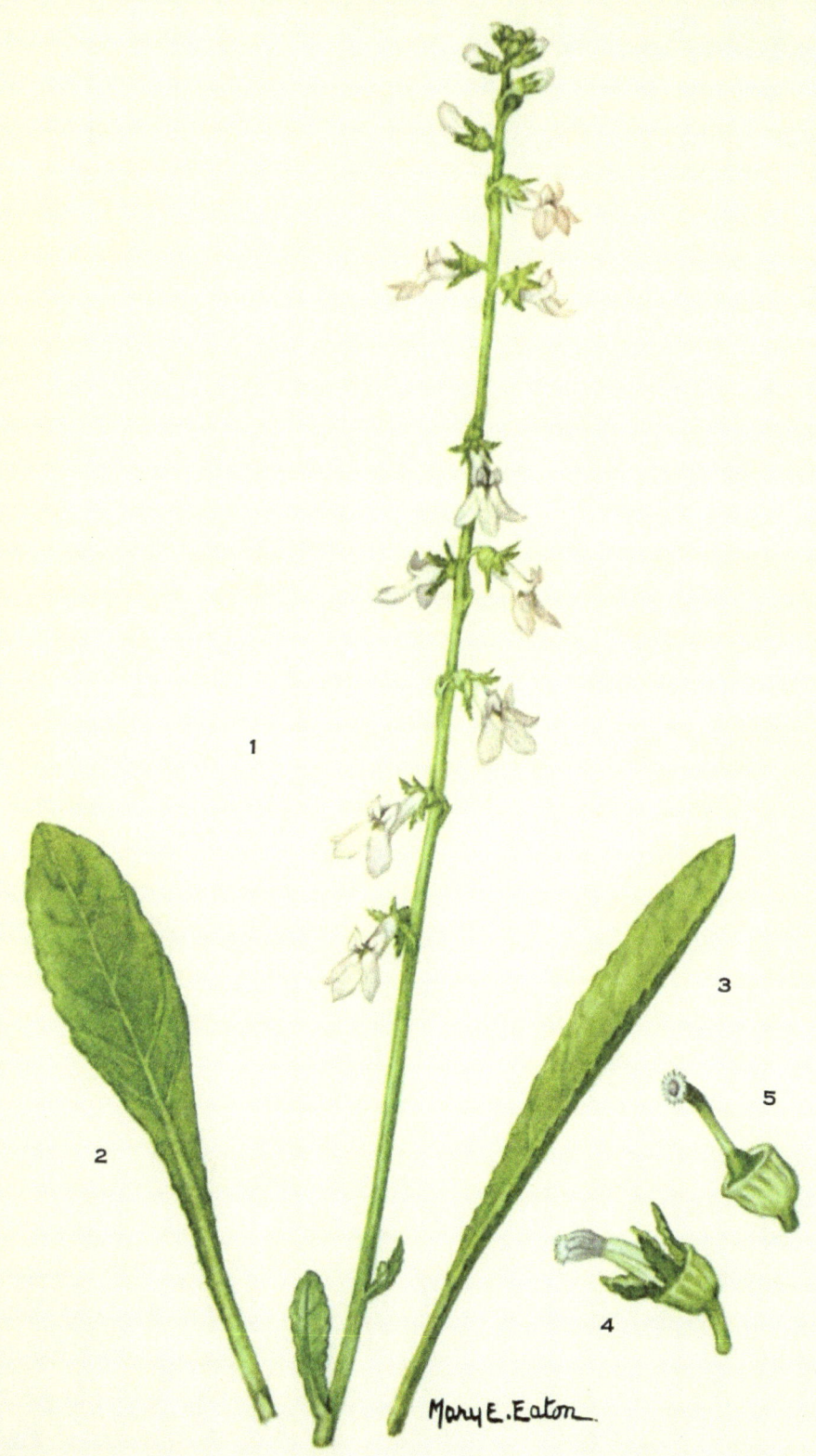

LOBELIA PALUDOSA

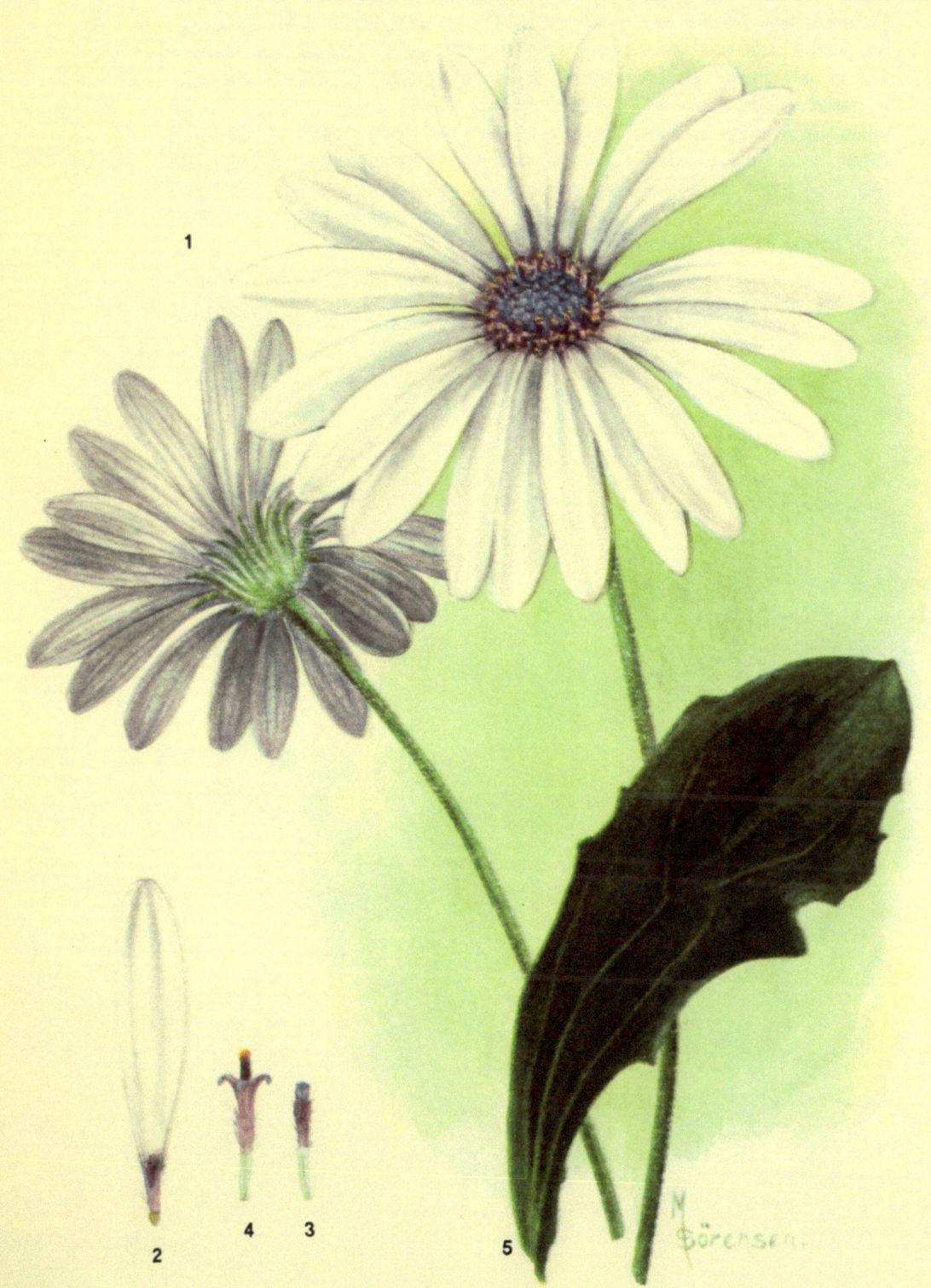

DIMORPHOTHECA ECKLONIS

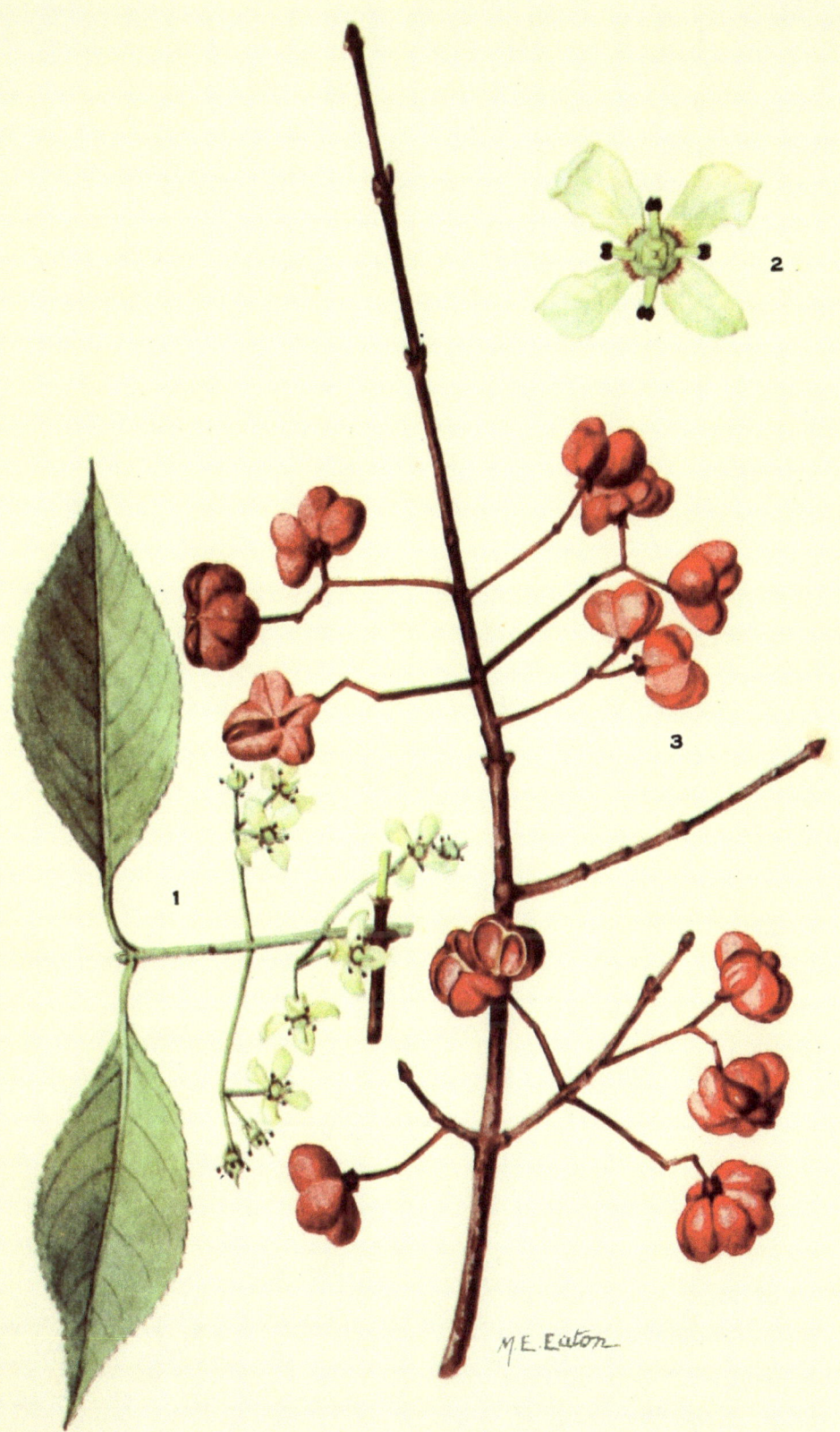

EUONYMUS BUNGEANUS

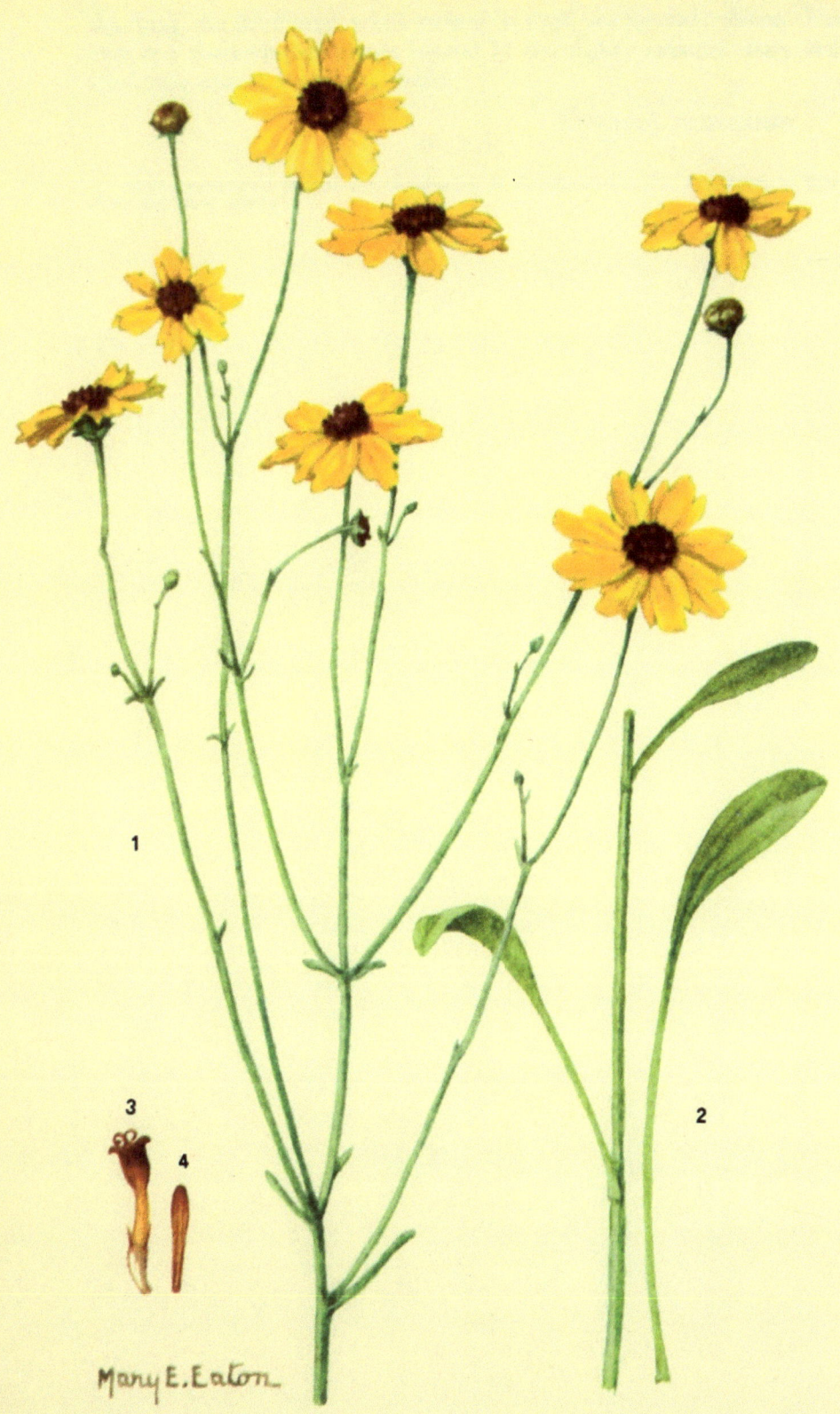

COREOPSIS LINIFOLIA

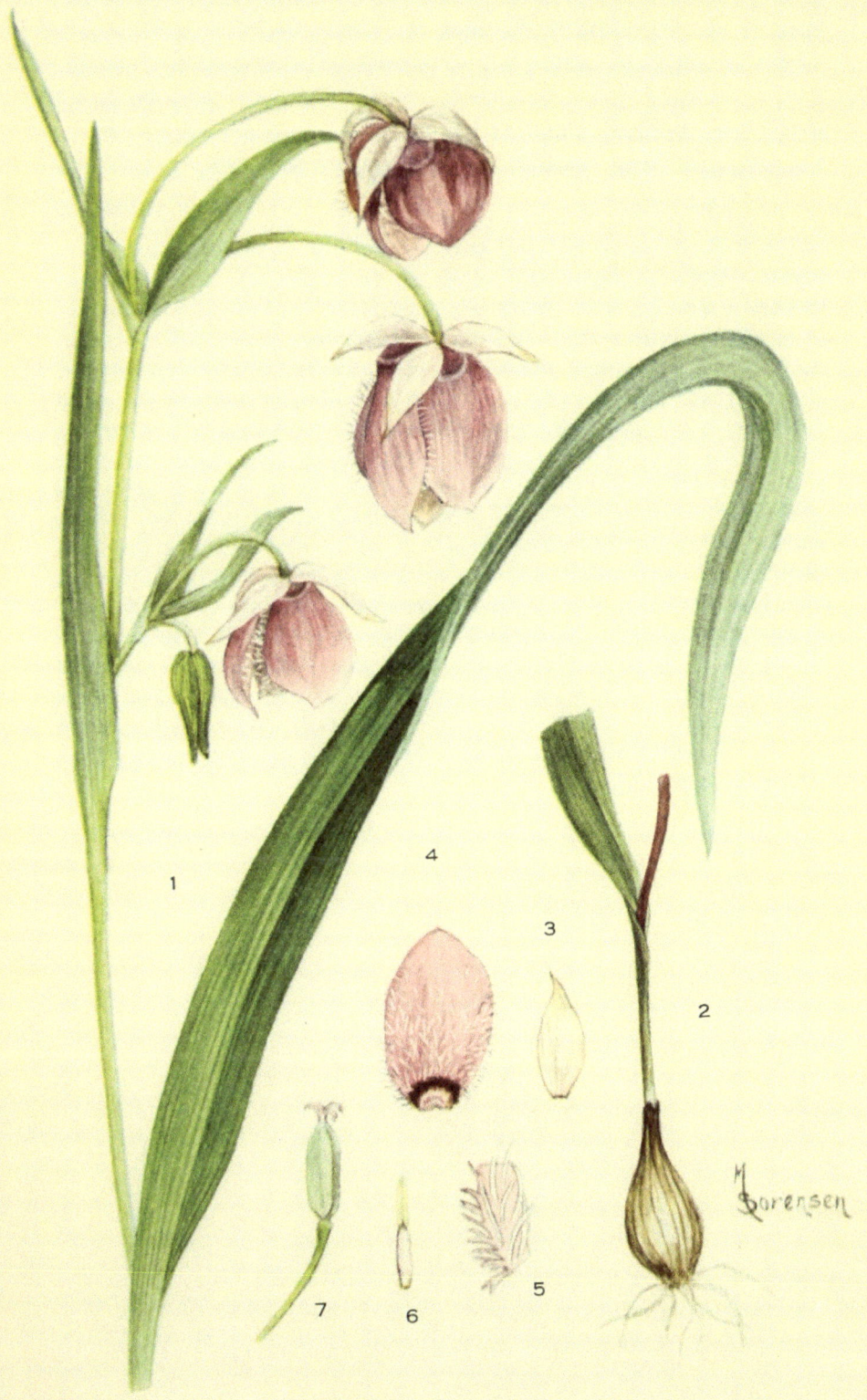

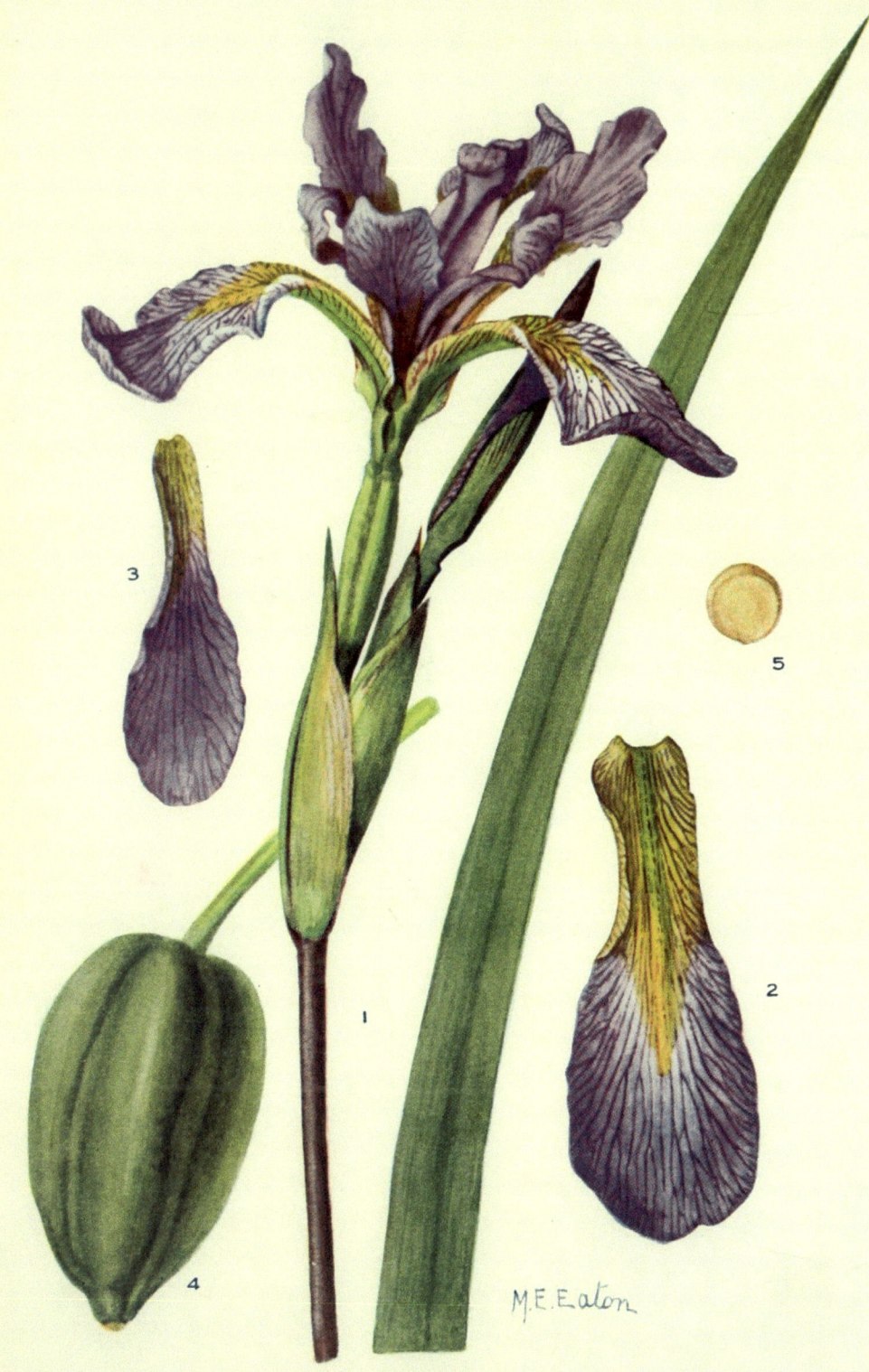

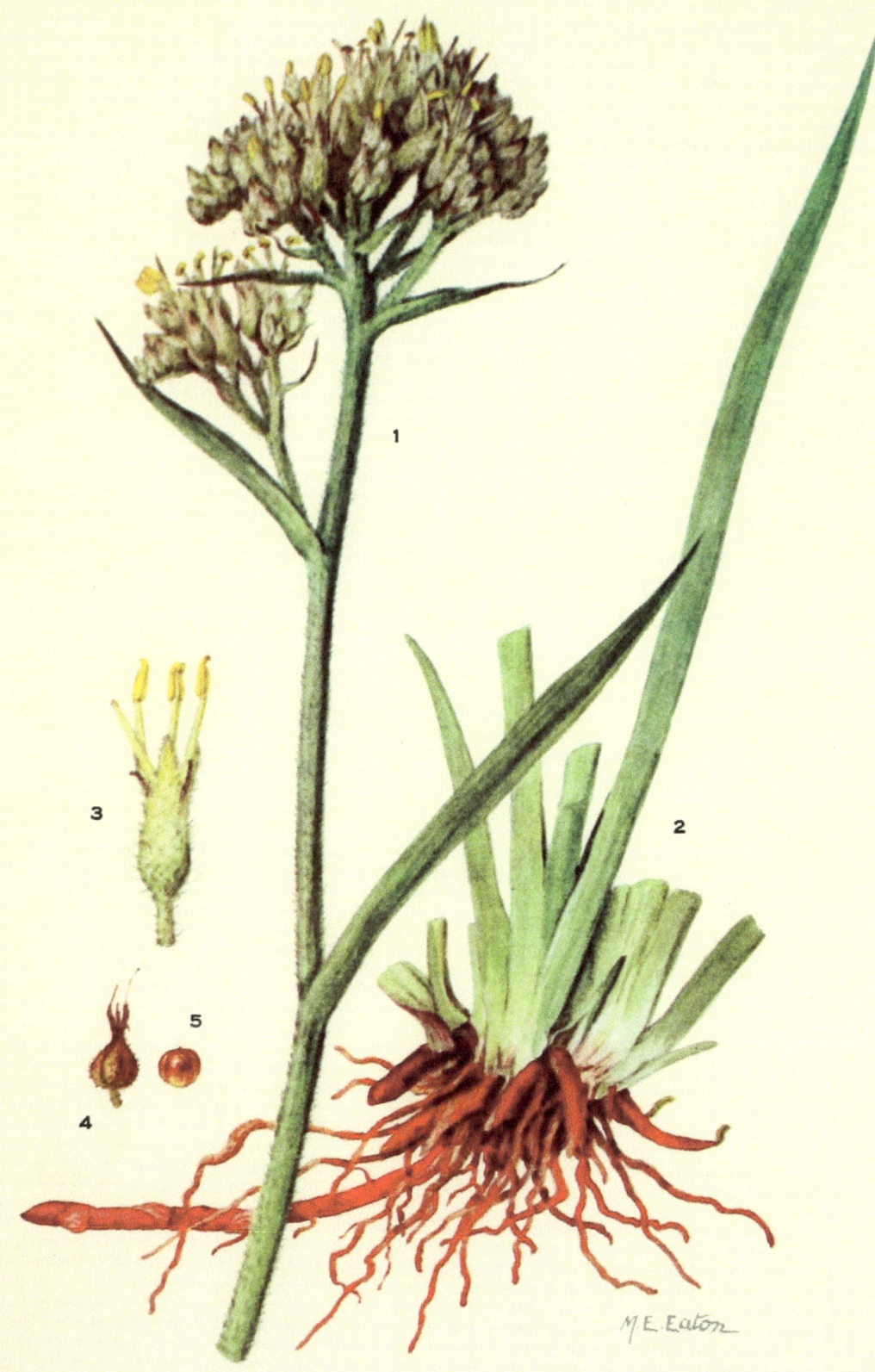

LACHNANTHES TINCTORIA

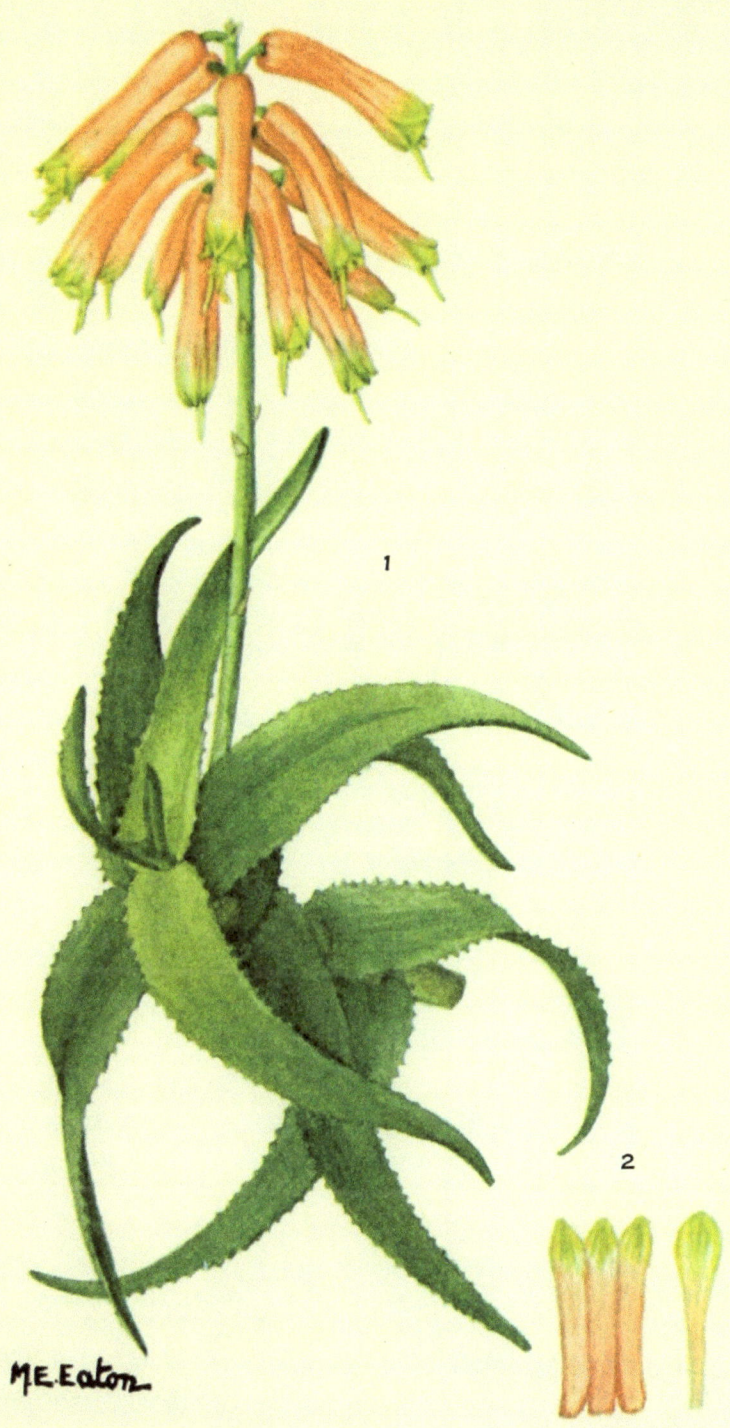

ALOË CILIARIS

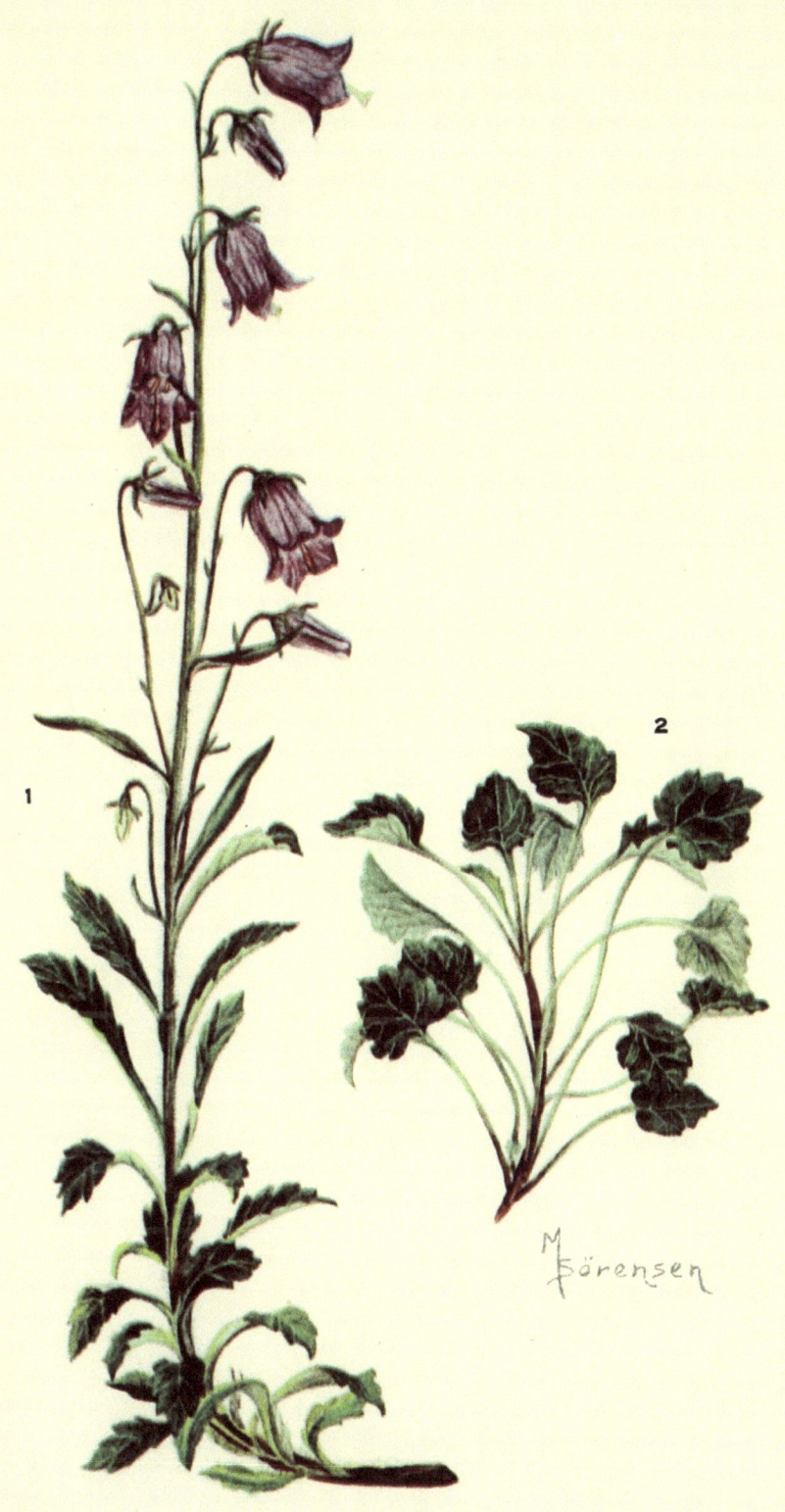

CAMPANULA COCHLEARIFOLIA

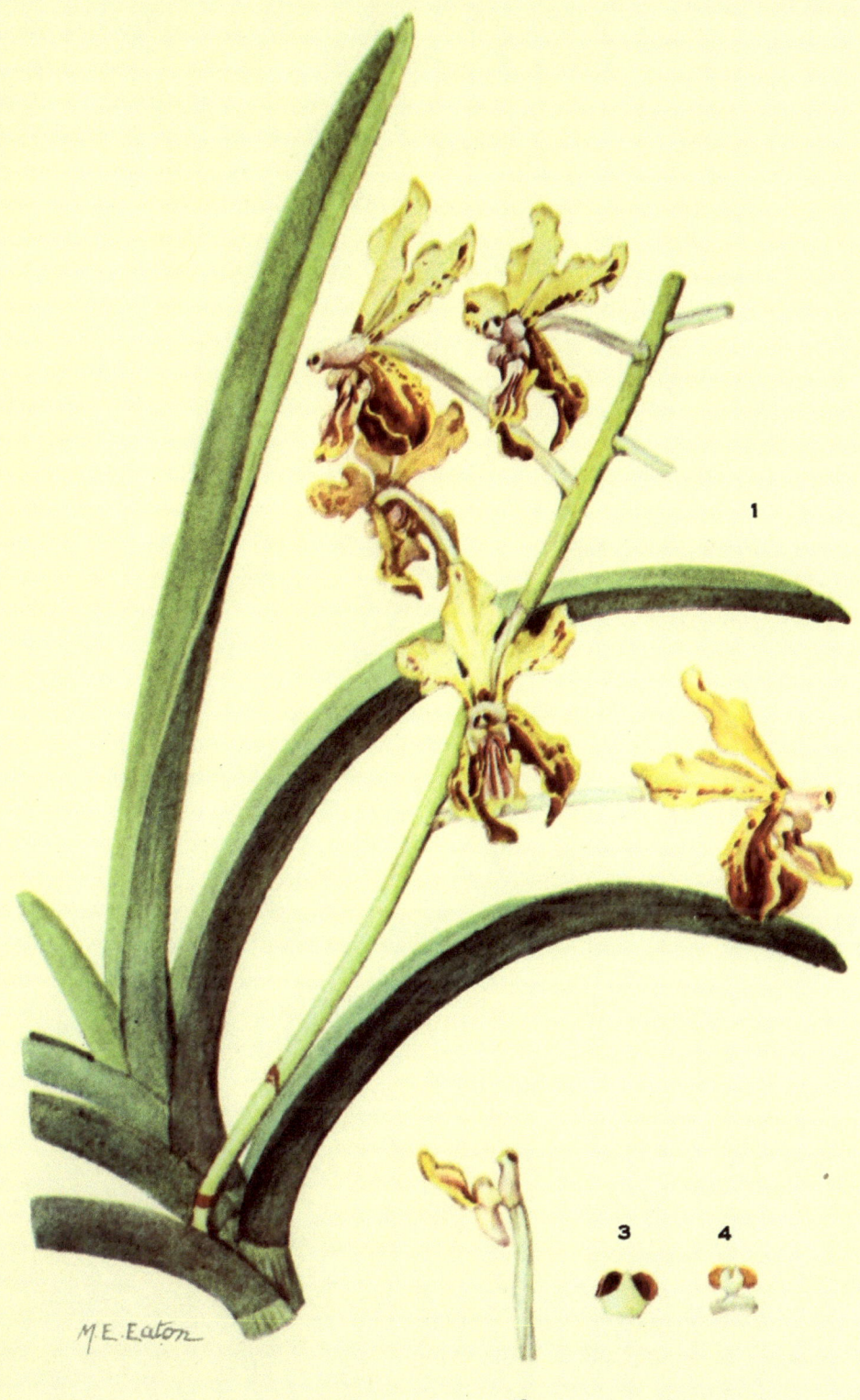

VANDA LAMELLATA

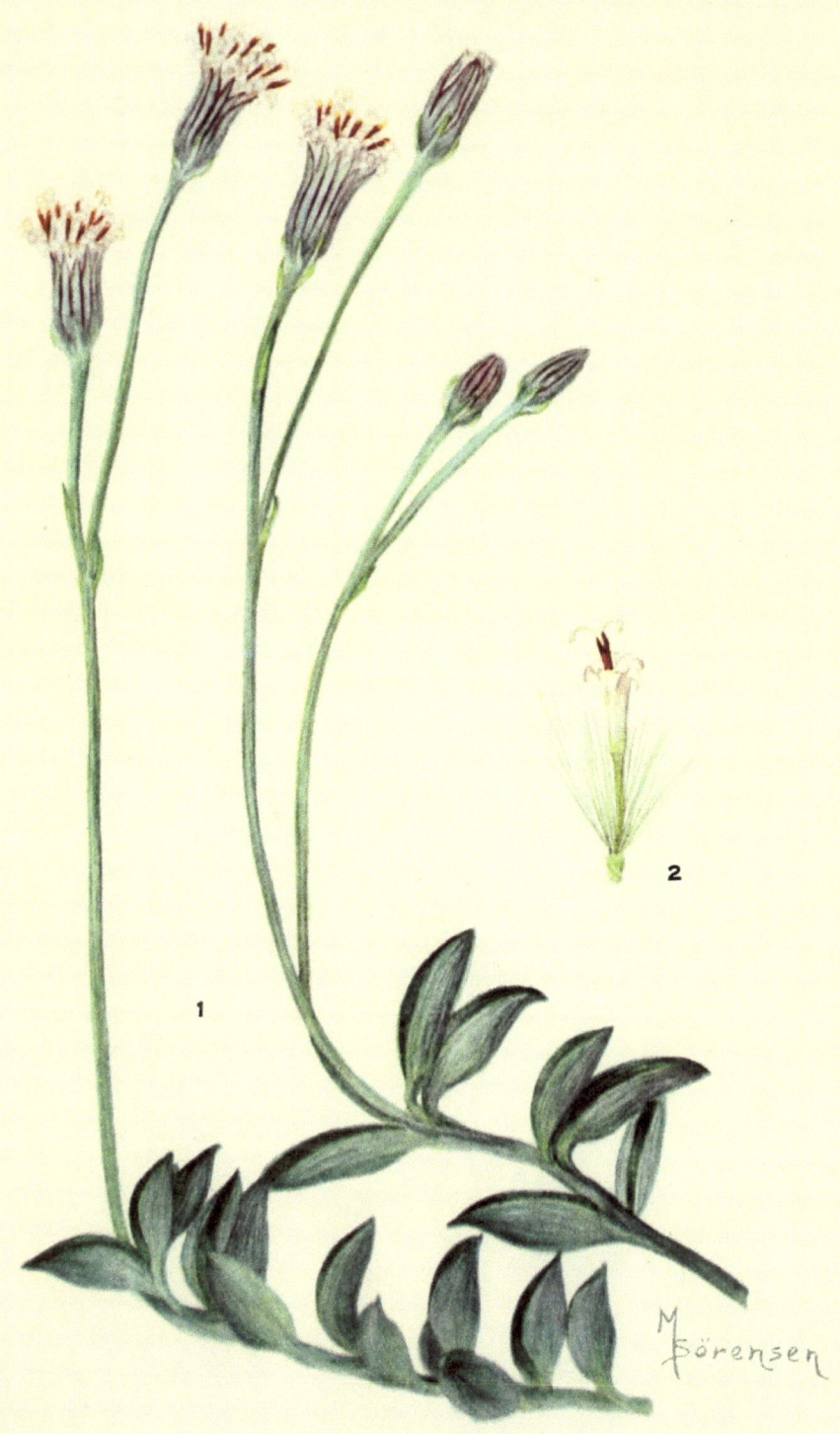

KLEINIA RADICANS

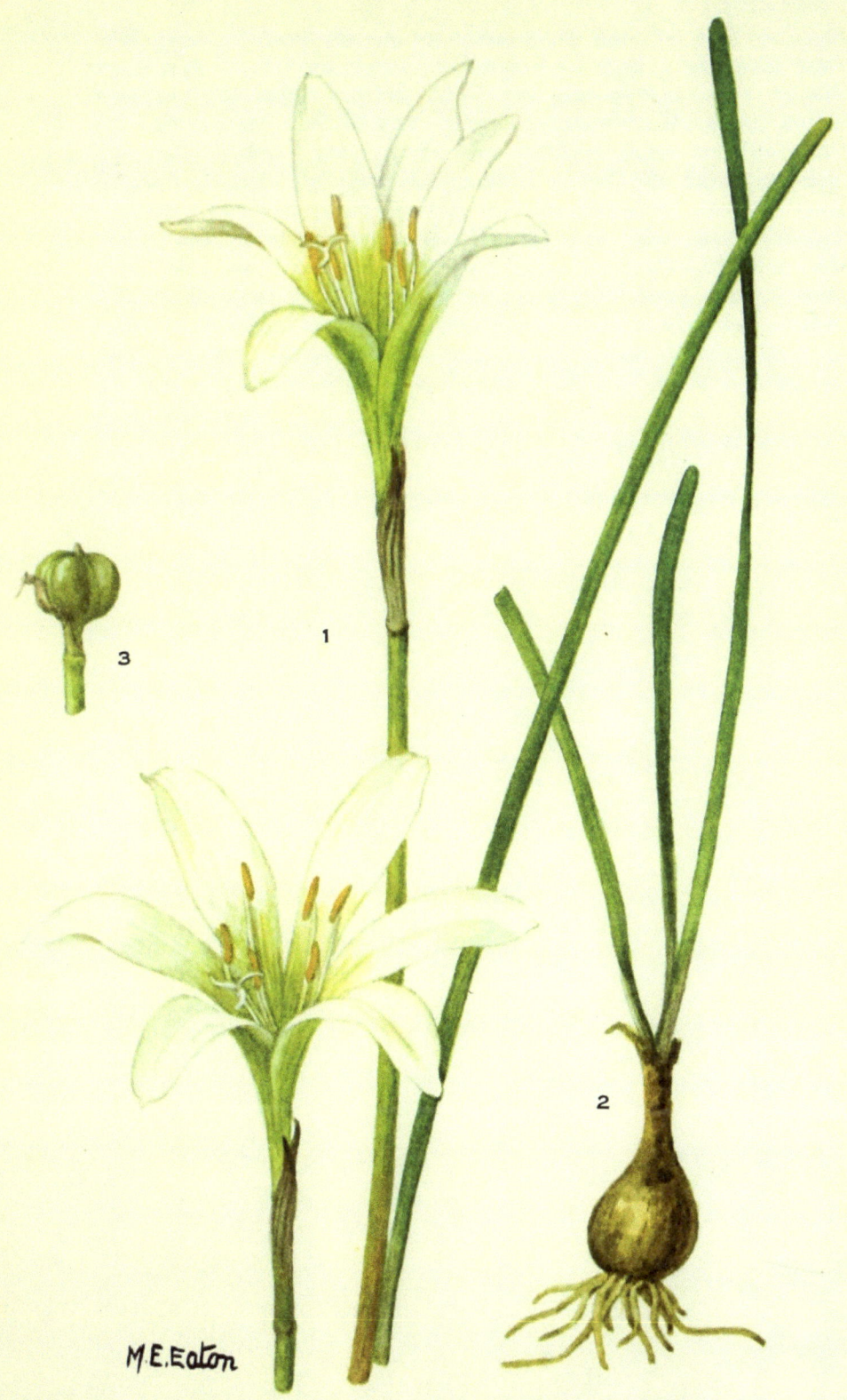

ZEPHYRANTHES TREATIAE

www.ingramcontent.com/pod-product-compliance
Lightning Source LLC
Chambersburg PA
CBHW040449220526
45473CB00004B/1568